VSB 192

MW00805445

LEONARD BERNSTEIN
ON THE TOWN

A MUSICAL COMEDY IN TWO ACTS

BOOK AND LYRICS BY
BETTY COMDEN AND ADOLPH GREEN

BOOK BASED ON AN IDEA OF JEROME ROBBINS

ADDITIONAL LYRICS BY LEONARD BERNSTEIN

ORCHESTRATIONS BY
LEONARD BERNSTEIN, HERSHY KAY, DON WALKER,
ELLIOTT JACOBY, TED ROYAL AND BRUCE COUGHLIN

LEONARD
BERNSTEIN
Music Publishing
Company LLC

BOOSEY & HAWKES

First publication for sale 1997, USA.

All rights of theatrical, radio and television performance, mechanical reproduction in any form whatsoever (including film), and translation of the libretto of the complete work, or parts thereof, are strictly reserved.

Cover Art/Design: Serino Coyne Inc.
Courtesy of Deutsche Grammophon, from the recording of ON THE TOWN,
conducted by Michael Tilson Thomas (CD: 437 516-2; Laser disc/VHS: 440 072 297-1/3)
Manufactured and Marketed by PolyGram Classics & Jazz, a Division of PolyGram Records, Inc., New York NY

LEONARD BERNSTEIN® is a registered trademark of The Amberson Group, Inc.

The Leonard Bernstein Music Publishing Company LLC,
is a venture of the Amberson Group and PolyGram Music Publishing.

∞ The paper used in this publication meets the minimum requirements of American National Standard for Information Sciences-Permanence of Paper for Printed Library Materials, ANSI Z39 48-1984

The engraving of this score is based on Leonard Bernstein's
conducting score for his 1960 Columbia recording of *On The Town*,
and the score and orchestra material used in the 1992
Deutsche Grammophon recording under Michael Tilson Thomas,
which was prepared with the participation of
Betty Comden and Adolph Green.

Charles Harmon and David Israel, editors;
With grateful acknowledgment for assistance in preparation of this score:

Finn Byrhard, of Hog River Music;

Dale Kugel, of Tams Witmark Music Library, Inc.;

Robert Wharton, of Boosey & Hawkes;

Michael Barrett, Sid Ramin, and Michael Tilson Thomas.

To Betty Comden and Adolph Green,
joyous, endearing, always inspired,
we owe special gratitude and affection.

Facsimile of composer's manuscript sketch to *I Feel Like I'm Not Out of Bed Yet,*
New York, New York, and (at bottom) *The Real Coney Island*

CONTENTS

	Page
About "On The Town" by Betty Comden and Adolph Green	ix
Characters and Vocal Ranges	x
Original Broadway production credits and cast list	xi
Michael Tilson Thomas recording credits and cast list	xii
Concert performance running order	xiii
Instrumentation	xiv

		Page
I.	Overture	1

Act I

Scene 1   **The Brooklyn Navy Yard**
2.	I Feel Like I'm Not Out Of Bed Yet (*Three Workmen and Men's Quartet*)	8
2a.	New York, New York (*Gabey, Chip and Ozzie*)	12

Scene 2   **A Subway Train in Motion**
2b.	Chase Music (*Instrumental*)	26

Scene 3   **A New York City Street**
3.	Gabey's Comin' (*Gabey, Chip, Ozzie and Women's Chorus*)	26

Scene 4   **Presentation of Miss Turnstiles**
4.	Presentation of Miss Turnstiles (Underscore, Vocal and Instrumental)(*Announcer and Ivy Smith*)	34
4a.	Chase Music (*Instrumental*)	46

Scene 5   **A Taxicab**
5.	Come Up To My Place (*Hildy and Chip*)	47
5a.	Chase Music (*Instrumental*)	61

Scene 6   **The Museum of Natural History**
6.	Carried Away (*Claire and Ozzie*)	62
6a.	Carried Away Encore (*Claire and Ozzie*)	72
6b.	Chase Music (*Instrumental*)	76

Scene 7   **A Busy New York City Street**
7.	Lonely Town (*Gabey*)	77
7a.	High School Girls (*Instrumental*)	84
7b.	Lonely Town Pas de Deux (*Instrumental*)	86
7c.	Lonely Town Choral (*Gabey and Chorus*)	89

Scene 8   **A Corridor and Studio in Carnegie Hall**
8.	Carnegie Hall Pavane (*Ivy Smith, Madame Dilly and Women's Chorus*)	94

Scene 9   **Claire's Apartment**
9.	I Understand (one verse) (*Pitkin*)	101
9a.	Carried Away Tag (*Claire and Ozzie*)	102

Scene 10   **Hildy's Apartment**
10.	I Can Cook Too (*Hildy*)	103
10a.	I Can Cook Too Encore (*Hildy*)	111

Scene 11   **Times Square**
11.	Lucky To Be Me (*Gabey and Chorus*)	115
11a.	Lucky To Be Me Incidental (*Underscore*)	121
12.	Times Square Ballet: Finale, Act I (*Instrumental*)	122

13.   Entr'acte   137

Act II

Scene 1A   Diamond Eddie's Nightclub
14.   So Long, Baby (*Diamond Eddie's Girls*)   142
15.   I Wish I was Dead (*Diana Dream*)   147
15a.   I Understand (recitative) (*Pitkin*)   149

Scene 1B   The Congacabana
16.   Conga Cabana (Instrumental Change of Scene)   149
17.   I Wish I was Dead (Spanish) (*Dolores Dolores*)   151
18.   Ya Got Me (*Hildy, Claire, Chip and Ozzie*)   153
18a.   Ya Got Me Encore (*Claire, Hildy, Chip and Ozzie*)   168
18b.   I Understand (recitative) (*Pitkin*)   170

Scene 1C   The Slam Bang Club
19.   Slam Bang Blues (Dixieland) (Instrumental Change of Scene)   170
20.   I Understand (Pitkin's Song) (*Pitkin*)   171
20a.   Chase Music (Instrumental)   175

Scene 2   The Subway Train to Coney Island
21.   Subway Ride and Imaginary Coney Island (Instrumental)   176

Scene 3   The Dream Coney Island
21a.   The Great Lover Displays Himself (Instrumental)   181
21b.   Pas de Deux (Instrumental)   187

Scene 4   Another Subway Train to Coney Island
22.   Some Other Time (*Claire, Hildy, Chip and Ozzie*)   192

Scene 5   The Real Coney Island
23.   The Real Coney Island (Instrumental, Underscore and Vocal) (*Rajah Bimmy*)   199

Scene 6   The Brooklyn Navy Yard
24.   Finale, Act II (*Gabey, Chip, Ozzie, Claire, Hildy, Ivy Smith, Three New Sailors and Entire Company*)   210

25.   Bow Music   218
26.   Exit Music   222

About *On The Town*

By the spring of 1944 our friend Leonard Bernstein had not only shot like a comet across the musical world, first substituting brilliantly for Bruno Walter, then creating with Jerome Robbins the landmark ballet *Fancy Free*, he had also saved two human lives—ours. Out in Hollywood our night-club act, The Revuers, had come to a dead-end street, La Finita, somewhere between El Desperando Boulevard and La Futura Nada. We were back in New York trying to rise phoenix-like from our own decimated ashes, as a two-act, at the Blue Angel. Leonard and Jerome, now at a dizzying peak through their first ballet, were about to use it as a springboard for a full-length musical comedy. Leonard suggested, to the incredulous, doubting, and crossed eyes and ears of all concerned, that we two write the book and lyrics. It was an act of pure faith and love. True, he had known us a long time, I (Betty) having met him when The Revuers began through me (Adolph), who had become his friend years before; and he knew and obviously valued our work; paying us the tribute of committing it in its entirety to memory, and making it part of his daily frame of reference. Something made him believe that although we had written only satirical numbers and sketches thus far, we would, at that point, be able to create a story, characters, and real songs. He was persuasive, and soon we were all working together on what became *On The Town*, in an atmosphere of exaltation, hilarity, and anticipation, balanced by despair, hopelessness, and wondering whether our first show would ever become a reality. There were not a few pursed lips about, expressing the thought that perhaps a Broadway show was an undignified sidetrack for Leonard, pulling him away from serious music. But to Leonard all music was serious. The distinction is not between "important" and "frivolous"; it is only between good and bad. His music for *On The Town* is unique in musical comedy history, and in his own as well, since it dramatizes a mainly comedic, contemporary (mid 20th-century) story in truly symphonic terms. We can hear our director George Abbott saying with hearty appreciation: "I just love that Pro-kaaaa-fieff stuff." That Pro-kaaaa-fieff stuff is pure Bernstein.

We may not have fully appreciated the full impact of that sound on opening night, because we were also in the show playing parts; and when Leonard came backstage he found two one-hundred-per-cent actors bemoaning a laugh they had missed in their big scene leading to "Carried Away." Leonard's excited face reassured the mummers and the writers as well that they would have another chance at that laugh. The show would surely still be running the next night.

We shall always be grateful to have had that joyous and creative experience with our genius friend who, back in '44, had had the faith to save us from being just a two-act, and to head us toward that street, La Futura Possible.

Betty Comden and Adolph Green
1995

Characters and Vocal Ranges

Singing Roles

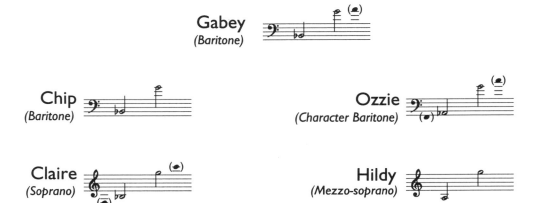

Gabey *(Baritone)*

Chip *(Baritone)*

Ozzie *(Character Baritone)*

Claire *(Soprano)*

Hildy *(Mezzo-soprano)*

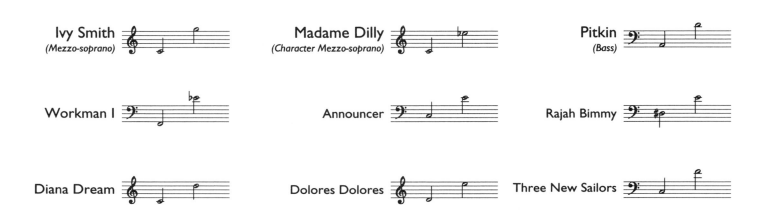

Ivy Smith *(Mezzo-soprano)*

Madame Dilly *(Character Mezzo-soprano)*

Pitkin *(Bass)*

Workman I

Announcer

Rajah Bimmy

Diana Dream

Dolores Dolores

Three New Sailors

Chorus: SATB

from the Chorus:

Navy Yard workmen, New York City girls, Singing Teachers, Times Square passersby, Diamond Eddie's Girls

Non-singing roles:

Second workman	Another policeman
Third workman	Professor Waldo Figment
Andy, a sailor	An actor
Tom, another sailor	First musician
Flossie	Second musician
Flossie's girl friend	Ballet girl
Subway bill poster	Ballet boy
Little old lady	First girl dancer
A policeman	Second girl dancer
Mr S Uperman	Lucy Schmeeler
A man	First waiter
Another man	Second waiter
A delicate type	Master of ceremonies
A girl	A girl

Prehistoric men, Bird girls, Nightclub patrons

Original Broadway Production Credits and Cast List

Oliver Smith and Paul Feigay presented *On The Town* on December 13, 1944, at the Colonial Theatre, Boston. The New York opening was December 28, 1944, at the Adelphi Theatre, with the following credits and cast:

ON THE TOWN

Music by Leonard Bernstein
Book and lyrics by Betty Comden and Adolph Green
Book based on an idea by Jerome Robbins
Additional lyrics by Leonard Bernstein

Orchestrations by Leonard Bernstein,
Hershy Kay, Don Walker, Elliott Jacoby and Ted Royal

Musical Numbers and Choreography staged by Jerome Robbins
Production designed by Oliver Smith
Costumes designed by Alvin Colt
Lighting by Sam Amdurs
Technical Director: Peggy Clark
Production Assistant: Peter Foster
Musical Director: Max Goberman

Production Directed by George Abbott

Workman	Marten Sameth
2nd Workman	Frank Milton
3rd Workman	Herbert Greene
Ozzie	Adolph Green
Chip	Cris Alexander
Sailor	Lyle Clark
Gabey	John Battles
Andy	Frank Westbrook
Tom	Richard D'Arcy
Flossie	Florence MacMichael
Flossie's Friend	Marion Kohler
Bill Poster	Larry Bolton
Little Old Lady	Maxine Arnold
Policeman	Lonny Jackson
S. Uperman	Milton Taubman
Hildy	Nancy Walker
Policeman	Roger Treat
Figment	Remo Bufano
Claire	Betty Comden
Highschool Girl	Nellie Fisher
Sailor in Blue	Richard D'Arcy
Maude P. Dilly	Susan Steell
Ivy	Sono Osato
Lucy Schmeeler	Alice Pearce
Pitkin	Robert Chisholm
Master of Ceremonies	Frank Milton
Singer	Frances Cassard
Waiter	Herbert Greene
Spanish Singer	Jeanne Gordon
The Great Lover	Ray Harrison
Conductor	Herbert Greene
Bimmy	Robert Lorenz

Dancers: Barbara Gaye, Lavina Nielsen, Atty Vandenberg, Dorothy McNichols, Cyprienne Gabelman, Jean Handy, Virginia Miller, Nelle Fisher, Royce Wallace, Allyn Ann McLerie, Malka Farber, Aza Bard, Ray Harrison, Frank Neal, Carl Ebrele, James Flashe Riley, Ben Piazza, Douglas Matheson, Duncan Noble, Frank Westbrook, John Butler, Richard D'Arcy, Lyle Clark.

Singers: Frances Cassard, Jeanne Gordon, Lila King, Frances Lager, Marion Kohler, Dorothy Johnson, Regina Owens, Shirley Ann Burton, Frank Milton, Roger Treat, Martin Sameth, Benjamin Trotman, Milton Taubman, Herbert Greene, Lonny Jackson, Melvin Howard, Sam Adams, Robert Lorenz.

Michael Tilson Thomas Recording

On The Town was performed in concert on 28 and 29 June, 1992 at the Barbican Centre, London, England, and recorded for Deutsche Grammophon (Alison Ames, executive producer; Pål Christian Moe, Co-Producer; Arend Prohmann, recording producer; Helmut Burk, Balance Engineer), and was released with the following credits and cast:

ON THE TOWN

Music by Leonard Bernstein
Book & Lyrics by Betty Comden and Adolph Green
Orchestrations by Leonard Bernstein and Hershy Kay,
Don Walker, Elliott Jacoby, Bruce Coughlin and Ted Royal
("Ain't Got No Tears Left": jazz trio arrangement by Michael Tilson Thomas)

London Voices
Chorus Master: Terry Edwards
London Symphony Orchestra
Associate Conductor and Pianist: Michael Barrett
(Pianist in "Ain't Got No Tears Left": Michael Tilson Thomas)
Artistic Consultant: Patricia Birch
Conductor and Music Director: Michael Tilson Thomas

CLAIRE . . . . Frederica von Stade

HILDY . . . . Tyne Daly

IVY. . . . . Marie McLaughlin

GABEY . . . . Thomas Hampson

CHIP . . . . Kurt Ollmann

OZZIE. . . . . David Garrison

PITKIN / FIRST WORKMAN / ANNOUNCER . . . . Samuel Ramey

MADAME DILLY . . . . Evelyn Lear

THE NIGHTCLUB SINGER . . . . Cleo Laine

DIANA DREAM . . . . Meriel Dickinson

TWO WORKMEN . . . . Lindsay Benson

Stewart Collins

THREE "NEW" SAILORS . . . . Lindsay Benson

Bruce Ogsten

Nicholas Sears

RAJAH BIMMY . . . . Adolph Green

· · ·

Video cassette: 440 072 297 - 3
Laserdisc: 440 072 297 - 1
CD: 437 516-2

This recording was awarded Grammies for best music theatre recording and for best music theatre video in 1994, by the National Academy of Recording Arts and Sciences.

CONCERT PERFORMANCE RUNNING ORDER, 1996 EDITION

(timings are from the Deutsche Grammophon recording;
in addition, there are forty minutes of narration for the entire work)

Act I
(43 minutes and 38 seconds of music)

		Duration in minutes:
1.	The Star-Spangled Banner (ending)*	0:30
2	I Feel Like I'm Not Out of Bed Yet	2:07
2a.	New York, New York	4:00
3.	Presentation of Miss Turnstiles	6:11
3a.	Chase Music	0:15
4.	Gabey's Comin'	2:06
5.	Come Up To My Place	3:09
5a.	Chase Music	0:15
6.	Carried Away	3:01
6a.	Chase Music	0:15
7.	Lonely Town	3:30
7a.	High School Girls	0:39
7b.	Lonely Town Pas de Deux	3:13
8.	Carnegie Hall Pavane	2:35
8a.	I Understand (one verse)	0:40
8b.	Carried Away Tag	0:14
9.	I Can Cook Too	3:03
9a.	I Can Cook Too Encore	1:00
10.	Lucky To Be Me	3:03
11.	Times Square Ballet: Finale, Act I	4:32

Act II
(36 minutes and 47 seconds of music)

12.	The Intermission's Great*	2:32
13.	So Long, Baby	1:02
14.	I Wish I Was Dead	0:55
14a.	I Understand (recitative)	0:05
15.	Conga Cabana	0:30
16.	I Wish I Was Dead (Spanish)	0:35
17.	Ya Got Me	3:55
17a.	I Understand (recitative)	0:05
18.	Slam Bang Blues (Dixieland)	0:30
19.	I Understand (Pitkin's Song)	2:44
20.	Subway Ride & Imaginary Coney Island	3:54
20a.	The Great Lover Displays Himself	1:33
20b.	Pas de Deux	3:08
21.	Some Other Time	4:30
22.	The Real Coney Island	2:59
23.	Finale, Act II	2:45
24.	Some Other Time Encore*	2:20

* Piano/vocal scores for these numbers appear in the chorus book, available from the Boosey & Hawkes rental library.

Instrumentation

Flute (doubling Piccolo)

Oboe (doubling English Horn)

3 Clarinets in B♭ (1st doubling Clarinet in E♭,

   2nd doubling Alto Saxophone,

   3rd doubling Bass Clarinet in B♭)

2 Horns in F

3 Trumpets in B♭

3 Trombones

Timpani

Percussion (1 player)*

Piano / Celesta

Violin A, B, C

Viola

Cello

Contrabass

*Snare Drum, Bass Drum, Tom-tom, High-Hat, Suspended Cymbal, Cowbell, Triangle, Temple Block, Tambourine, Ratchet, Slide Whistle, Xylophone, Glockenspiel, Vibraphone.

Duration
Act I: 90 minutes
Act II: 50 minutes

For first class productions worldwide, contact the authors through Amberson, Inc.

For stock and amateur productions in the USA and Canada,
performance materials are available from the Tams Witmark Music Library.
For all other territories, performance materials are available from Boosey & Hawkes.

For concert performances and for performances of individual numbers worldwide,
performance materials are available from Boosey & Hawkes.

ON THE TOWN
1. Overture

Lyrics by
Betty Comden and Adolph Green

Music by
Leonard Bernstein

© Copyright 1977 by Warner Bros., Inc.
Leonard Bernstein Music Publishing Company LLC, Publisher.
Boosey & Hawkes, Inc. Sole Agent.
All rights reserved. International Copyright Secured.

VSB 192

Engraved and printed in U.S.A. 1997

4

Applause Segue

ACT ONE

2. I Feel Like I'm Not Out Of Bed Yet

Three Workmen and Men's Quartet

Segue

2a. New York, New York

Gabey, Chip and Ozzie

Enter three sailors (GABEY, CHIP, OZZIE)

B

OZZIE: Come on, Gabey, hurry up!   CHIP: Twenty-four hours! *(Gabey bumps into another sailor as he looks around.)*

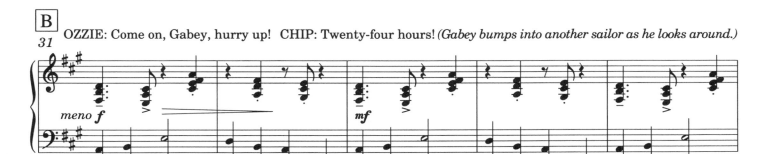

SAILOR: Hey, why don'tcha look where ya goin'? You'd think it was your first time in New York!   GABEY: It *is!*

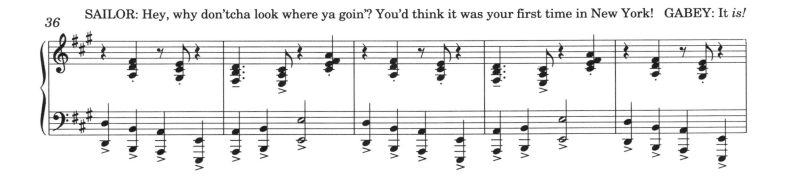

14

streets in New York City, not counting MacDougall Alley in the heart of Green-Witch Village, a charming thoroughfare filled with..." OZZIE (*interrupting*): Here we go again! You and your guidebook!

(GABEY): Tom and Andy!   OZZIE: Hey, Tom! Andy! Hey, fellas, how are the New York dames?

ANDY: Wonderful -- I don't remember a thing!   TOM: Awful! I remember everything!

(Tom and Andy exit.)

Man - hat - tan wom - en are dressed in silk and sa - tin,   Or so the

(Scene segues to a New York City street.)

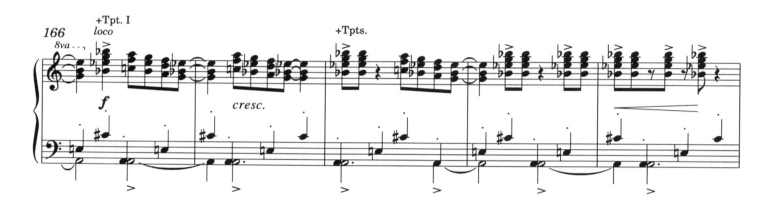

2b. Chase Music
Instrumental

Cue: LITTLE OLD LADY: Vandals! Vandals! Police!

3. Gabey's Comin'

Gabey, Chip, Ozzie and Women's Chorus

Cue: OZZIE: Yeah. Gabey's coming.

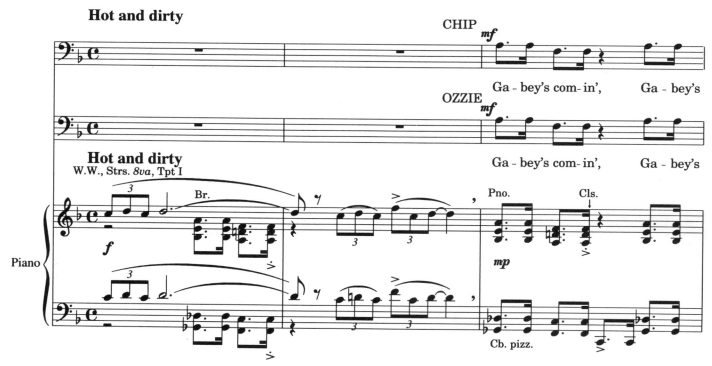

Chip: com - in' to town!_   He's on the town!_   With a day to burn, You're gon-

Ozzie: com - in' to town!_   He's on the town!_   With a day to burn, You're gon-

GABEY: Ga - bey's com-in' to town!_

Chip: na turn New York Ci - ty_ up - side_ down!_ Ga - bey's com-in' to town!_

Ozzie: na turn New York Ci - ty_ up - side_ down!_ Ga - bey's com-in' to town!_ Here's the way you do it!

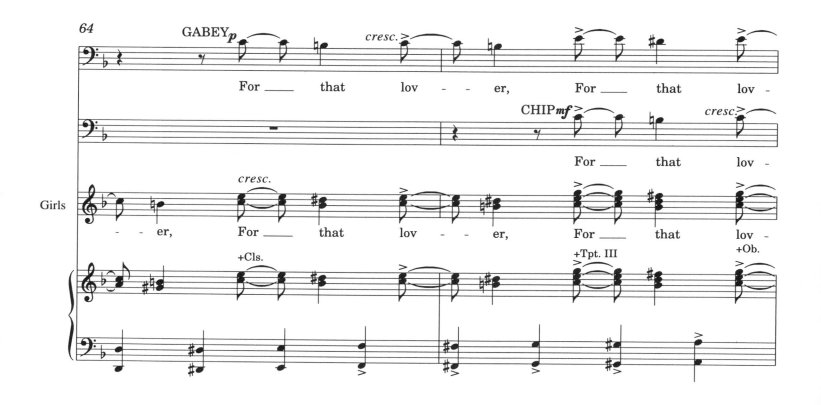

4. Presentation of Miss Turnstiles
Underscore, Vocal and Instrumental
Announcer and Ivy Smith

Cue: GABEY: To win such a title -- Miss Turnstiles for June.

ANNOUNCER:
Miss Turnstiles for June!

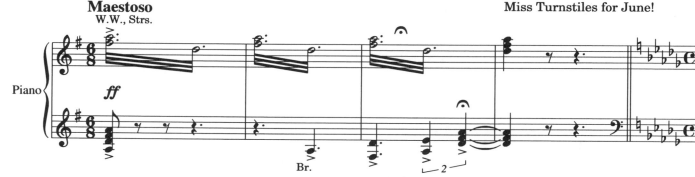

A

ANNOUNCER *(First time):* Every month, some lucky little New York miss
(Second time): There are 5,683 women who ride the subway every day.

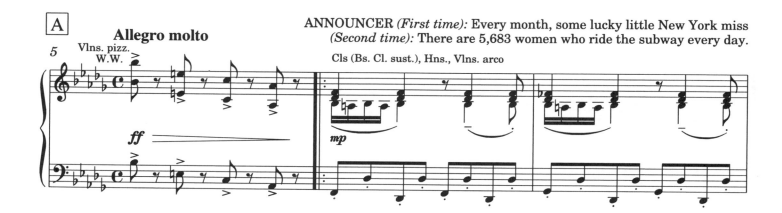

is chosen Miss Turnstiles for the month. She's got to be beautiful, she's got to be just an average girl, and most
And which fortunate lassie will be picked this month for the signal honor?

important of all, she's got to ride the subway.

GIRL: Who, me?
ANNOUNCER: Yes, you!
Ivy Smith! **B**

C **Allegretto di "Ballet Class"**

po - e - try and po - lo she's swell.

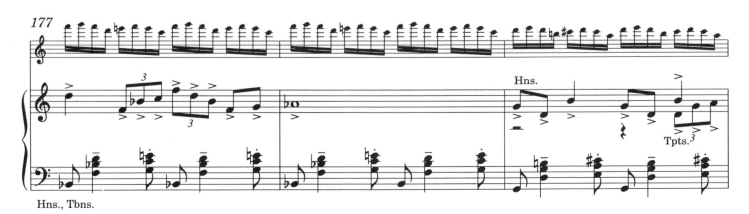

P

180

W.W., Tpts., Vlns.

Tbns., Perc.

W.W., Hns., Pno., Strs.

183

Tutti

W.W., Hns., Pno., Strs.

Tutti

186

8va

loco

ANNOUNCER: But of course at the end
of each month a new Miss
Turnstiles is chosen...

189

Applause Segue

4a. Chase Music
Instrumental

5. Come Up To My Place

Hildy and Chip

Cue: HILDY: Where d'ya wanna go first?!
(She starts the cab with a lurch.)

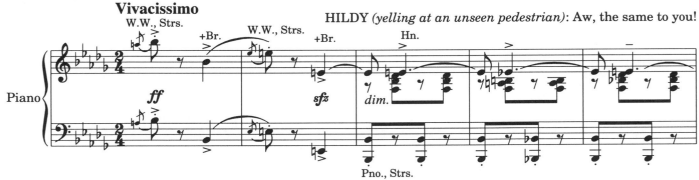

(Hildy puts the cab in gear.)

35 Chip: Oh, no, lady; I'd rather see the Forrest The-a-ter.

Repeat until Cue

W.W., Strs.

+Br.

ff

38 W.W., Strs.

+Br.

Hn.

sfz

p sub.

Pno., Strs.

42 **D**

CHIP

When I was home I saw the plays The La - dies' Dra - ma

Fl. with voice

E.Hn.

pp

46 Chip: Cir - cle showed. Now I am here I want to get Some tick - ets for "To -

Bs. Cl. with voice

(Hildy puts the cab back in gear again.)

71 Chip: No, could we go to Battery Park.

Repeat until Cue

74

G

78 CHIP: Back home I dreamt of catch-ing fish So big I could-n't

82 Chip: car-ry 'em. They told me that they have my size Right here in the A-

rit. molto

Hildy: My place! My place! My place! _____ My place!

Chip: Flat - iron Buil - ding! Hip - po - drome! ___

Applause Segue

5a. Chase Music
Instrumental

6. Carried Away

Claire and Ozzie

Cue: CLAIRE: Claire - another demerit.

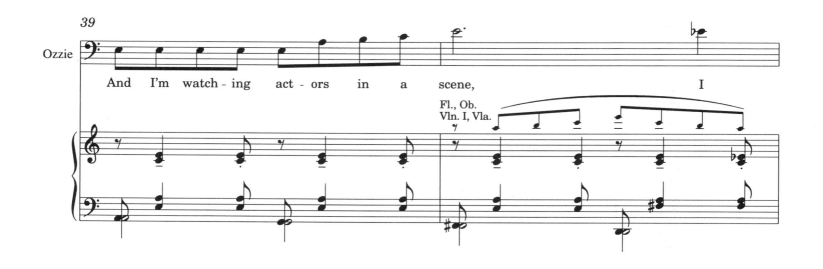

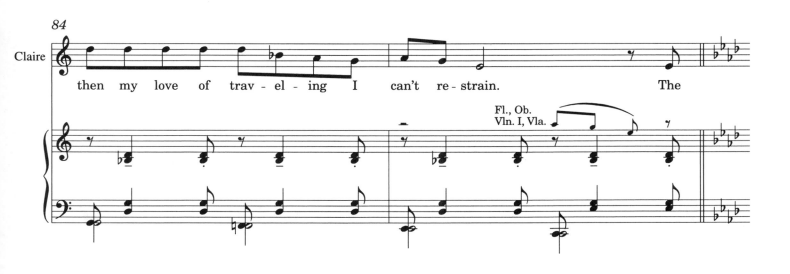

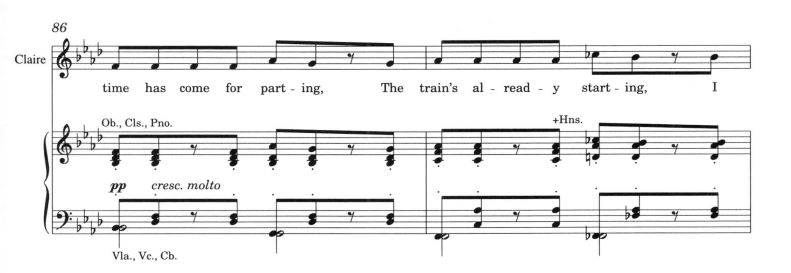

6a. Carried Away Encore
Claire and Ozzie

A **poco più presto**

15

Claire — I take an - thro - pol - o - gy so lit - 'ral - ly,

17

Claire — that these mod - ern days are not for me. Right

19

Claire — now I feel we're liv - ing pre - his - tor - ic - 'lly; To

21

Claire — us the past has beck - oned, We're go - ing back this sec - ond To

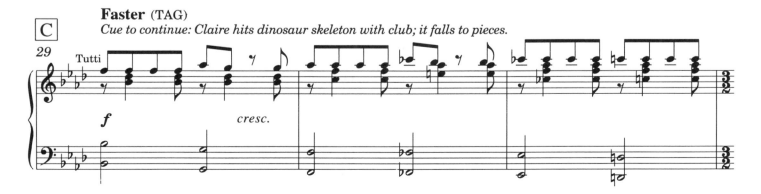

Applause Segue

6b. Chase Music
Instrumental

Applause Segue

7. Lonely Town

Gabey

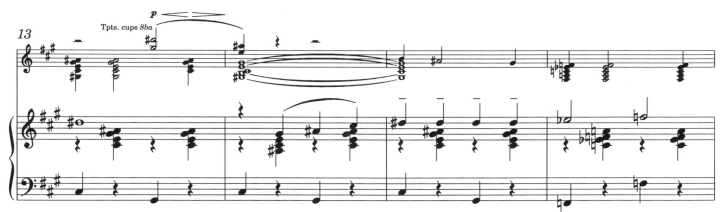

* In concert, this number begins at bar 27

GABEY: I beg your pardon, can you tell me where Carnegie Hall is?

GABEY: I beg your pardon...

82

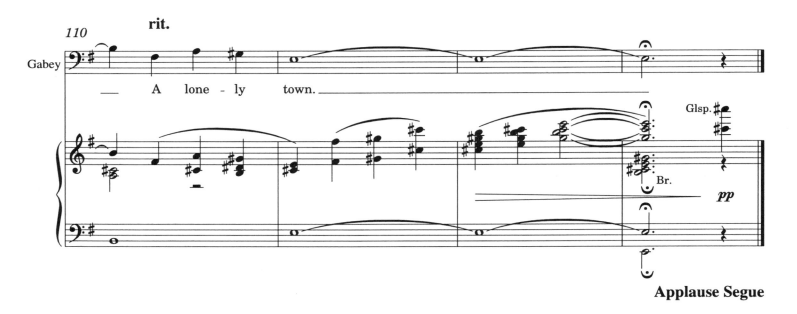

Applause Segue

7a. High School Girls
Instrumental

7b. Lonely Town
Pas de Deux

Instrumental

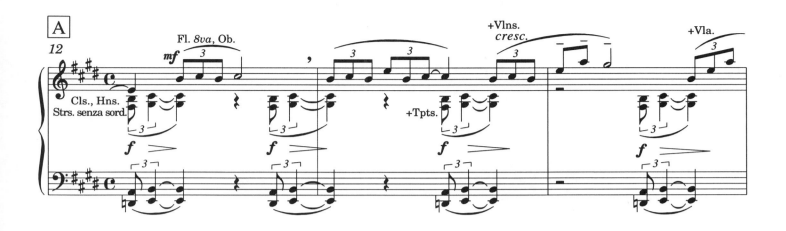

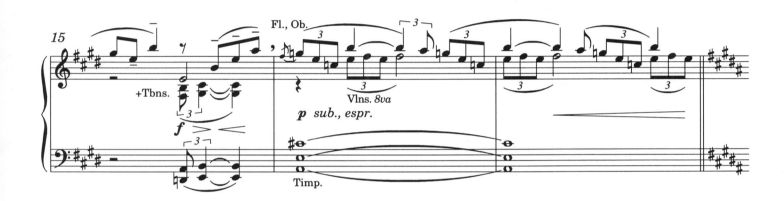

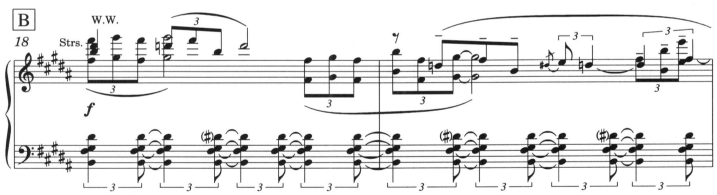

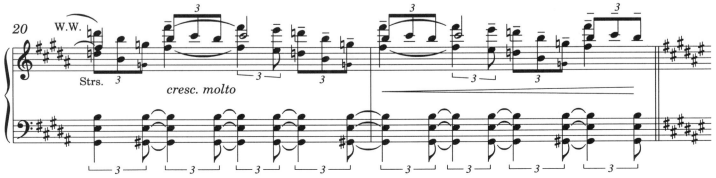

7c. Lonely Town Choral

Gabey and Chorus

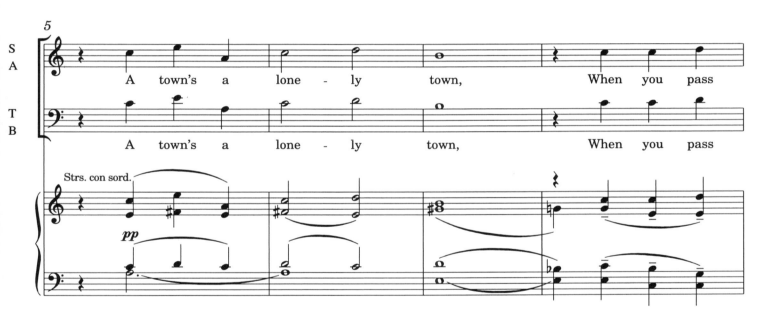

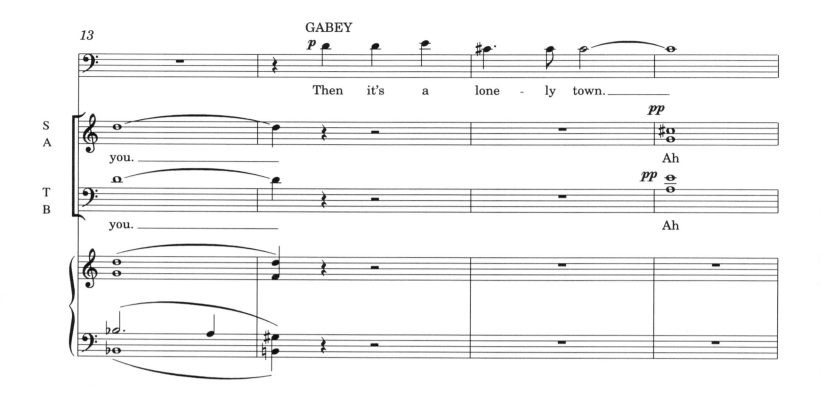

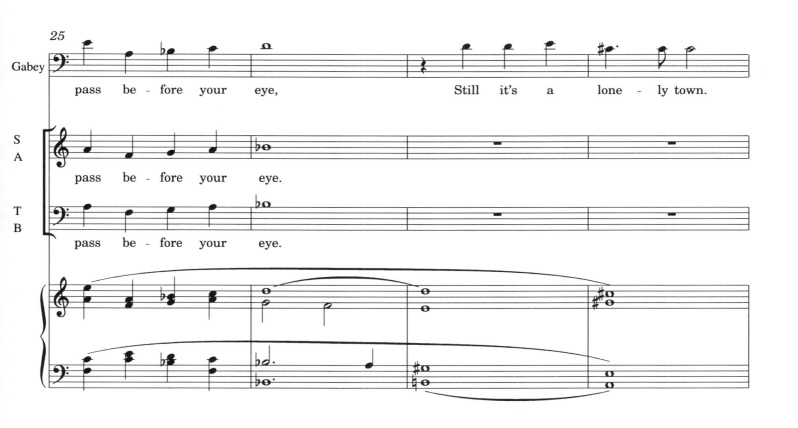

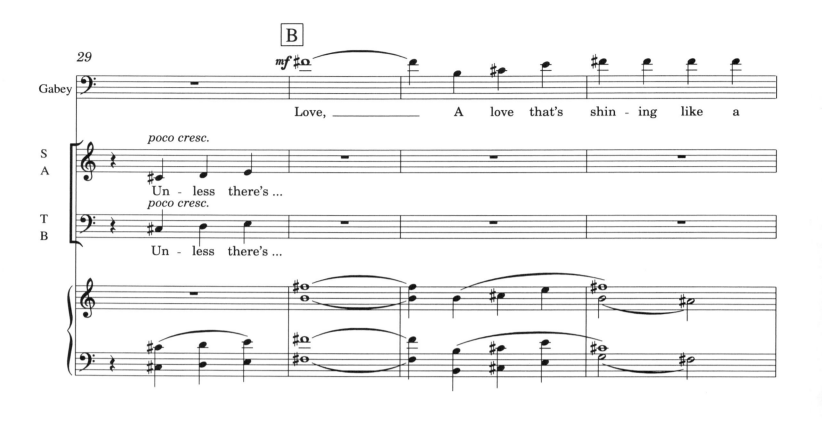

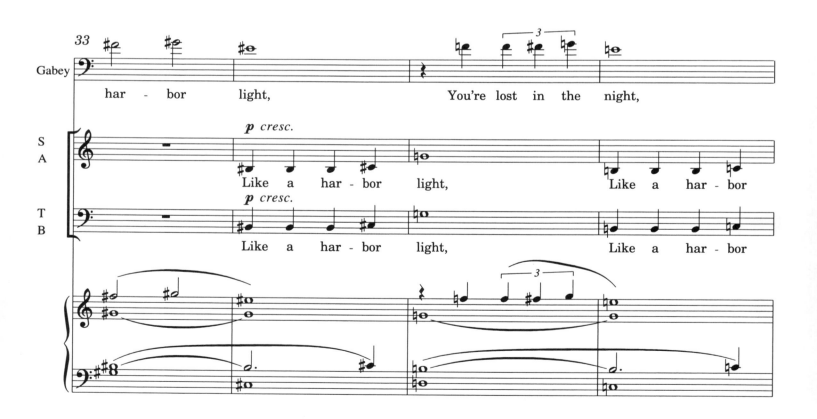

8. Carnegie Hall Pavane

Ivy Smith, Madame Dilly and Women's Chorus

Cue: MADAME DILLY: Now, your vocalise.

*In the original production, bars 35-48 were repeated.

9. I Understand

(one verse)
Pitkin

Cue: PITKIN: No sordid details, Claire. I understand.

Moderato, lugubriously

9a. Carried Away Tag

Claire and Ozzie

Cue: CLAIRE: Pitkin believes in the honor system.

10. I Can Cook Too

Hildy

Cue: CHIP: What's the specialty of the house? HILDY: Me!

Applause Segue

10a. I Can Cook Too Encore

Hildy

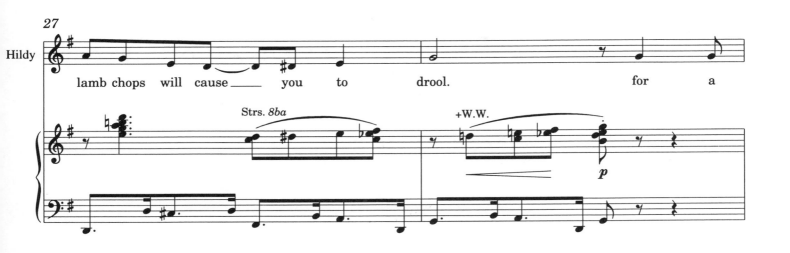

11. Lucky to Be Me

Gabey and Chorus

Cue: GABEY: She'll be here in half an hour.

116

E
46
a tempo
Gabey
me.
SOPRANOS & ALTOS unis.
mp
What a day, For- tune smiled and came my way, Bring - ing love I
TENORS & BASSES unis.
mp
What a day, For- tune smiled and came my way, Bring - ing love I
mp Cls. sust.
Tbns.
50
S
A
nev - er thought I'd see, I'm so luck - y to be me.
T
B
nev - er thought I'd see, I'm so luck - y to be me.
Fl., Ob. & Tpts. 8ba
Fl., Ob.
fp
Tbn. III, Cb.
F
54
S
A
mf
What a night, Sud - den - ly you came in sight, Look - ing just the
T
B
mf
What a night, Sud - den - ly you came in sight, Look - ing just the
mf
Tbns.

11a. Lucky to Be Me Incidental
Underscore

12. Times Square Ballet: Finale, Act I

Cue: CHIP: This town belongs to the Navy!   Instrumental

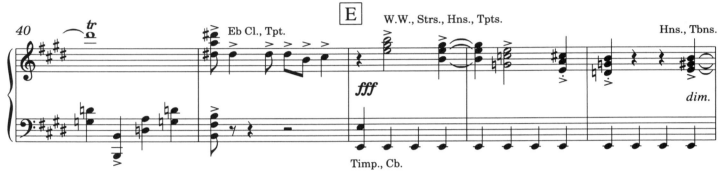

K

113

116

119

L

123

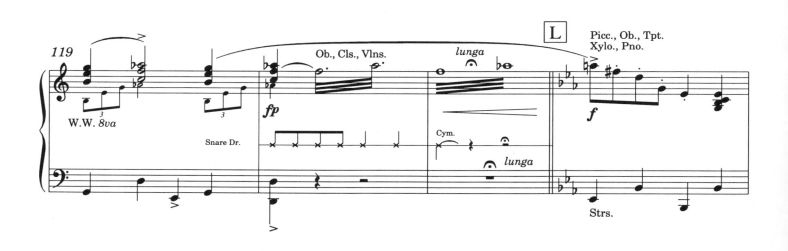

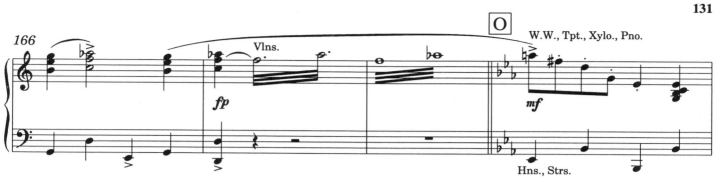

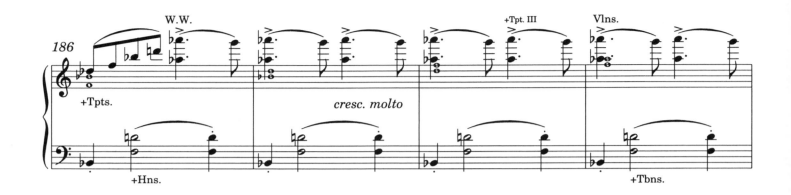

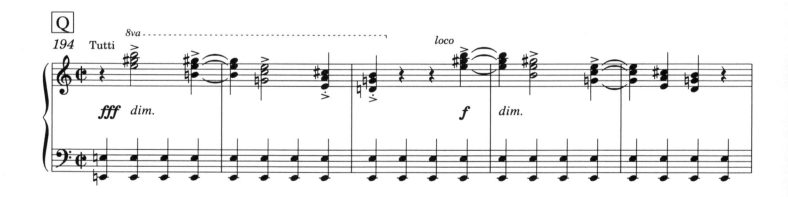

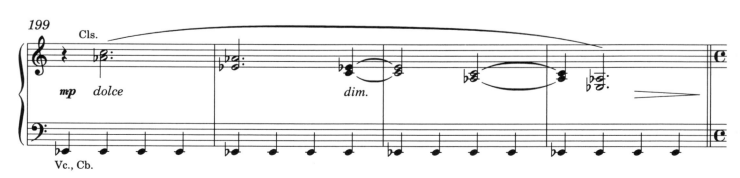

END OF ACT ONE

13. Entr'acte

Free and flowing

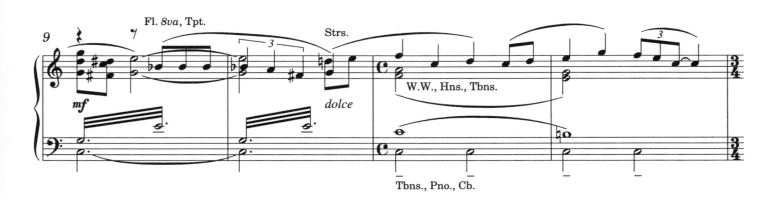

Applause Segue

ACT TWO

14. So Long, Baby

Diamond Eddie's Girls

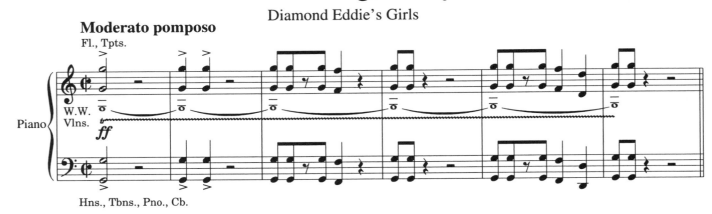

Cls.

Strs., Tpts., Pno.

GIRLS

I've got wise to you!

Cls., Pno., Vln.

TAG
Faster

Cls.

Tpts.

Tutti

Choke Cym.

15. I Wish I Was Dead

Diana Dream

Cue: MASTER OF CEREMONIES: Miss Diana Dream!

15a. I Understand
(recitative)
Pitkin

Cue: PITKIN: That's quite all right, darling.

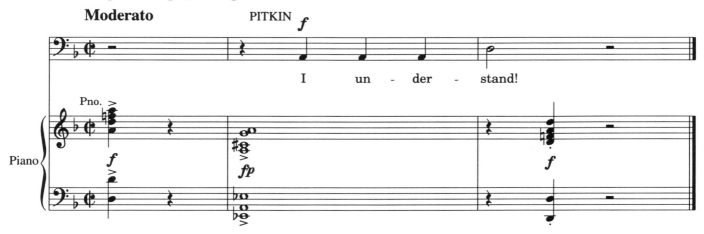

I un - der - stand!

16. Conga Cabana
Instrumental Change of Scene

Cue: CLAIRE: We're off to the Congacabana.

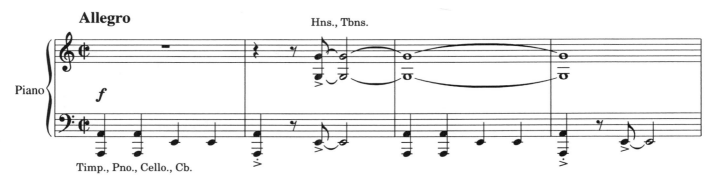

17. I Wish I Was Dead (Spanish)

Dolores Dolores

Cue: MASTER OF CEREMONIES: ...Señorita Dolores Dolores. Give her a nice hand.

guess I just don't rate with you, __ I veesh I was

daad _____ and

Repeat from A *as needed.*

Cut-off cue: HILDY: I'm awfully sorry, but my friend's allergic to that song.
(Dialogue continues)

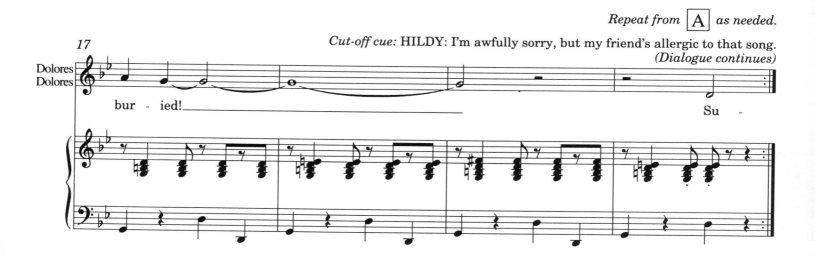

bur - ied! _____ Su -

18. Ya Got Me

Hildy, Claire, Chip and Ozzie

Cue: GABEY: They're trying to cheer me up.

113 CLAIRE & HILDY unis.

It's all free, it's all free, it's all free.

Chip

free. It's all free, it's all free, it's all free.

OZZIE

It's all free, it's all free, it's all free.

Strs.

Tutti

f

H

117 Br.

+W.W., Tpts., Strs. *8va*

120

ff Hns., Tbns. *f*

123

18a. Ya Got Me Encore

Claire, Hildy, Chip and Ozzie

18b. I Understand
(recitative)
Pitkin

Cue: CLAIRE: I was supposed to meet you here, wasn't I?
PITKIN: Darling,

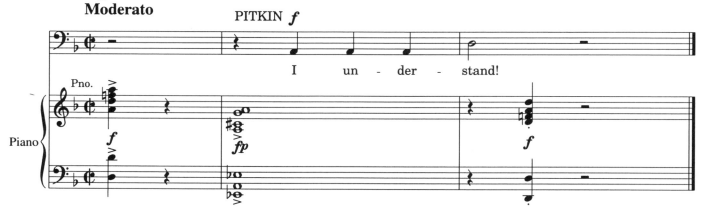

19. Slam Bang Blues (Dixieland)
Instrumental Change of Scene

Cue: CLAIRE: O.K. On to the Slam Bang!

20. I Understand (Pitkin's Song)

Pitkin

Cue: PITKIN: I always have.

20a. Chase Music
Instrumental

Cue: LUCY: Call me Lucy.

Segue

21. Subway Ride and Imaginary Coney Island
Instrumental

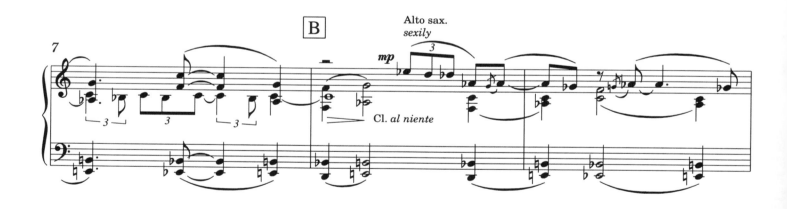

Repeat ad lib. (if necessary)

Twice as fast
W.W., Pno.

attacca

21a. The Great Lover Displays Himself
Instrumental

MASTER OF CEREMONIES: Good evening, ladies and gentlemen.
(Dialogue continues)

Segue

21b. Pas de Deux

Instrumental

Cue to continue: MASTER OF CEREMONIES:
Gabey the Great Lover versus Ivy Smith!

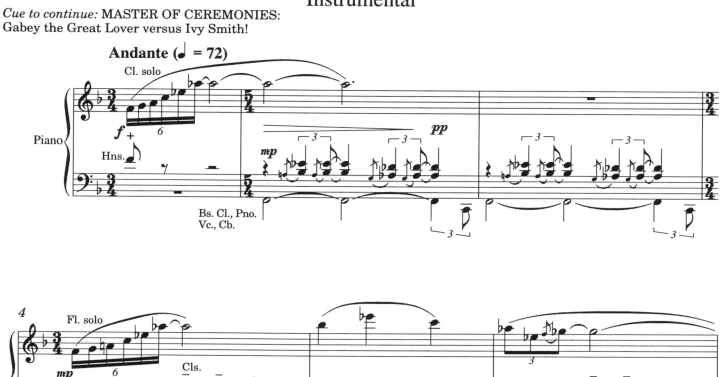

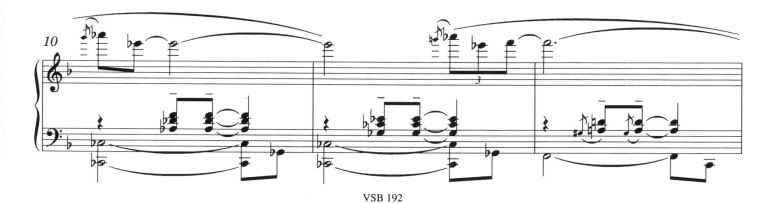

22. Some Other Time

Claire, Hildy, Chip and Ozzie

SUBWAY CONDUCTOR: Coney Island. All out.

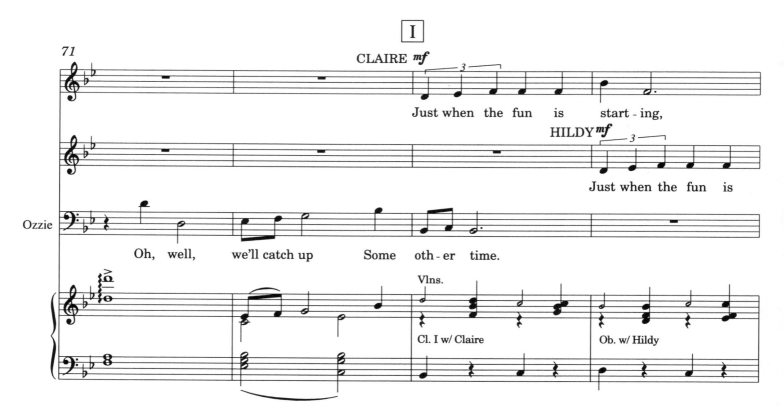

Applause Segue

23. The Real Coney Island

Instrumental, Underscore and Vocal

Rajah Bimmy

K RAJAH BIMMY: Hurry,

hurry, hurry! (Dialogue continues)

Cut-off cue: GABEY: Ivy! IVY: Gabey! *(Dialogue continues)*

24. Finale, Act II

Gabey, Chip, Ozzie, Claire, Hildy, Ivy Smith,
Three New Sailors and Entire Company

D Allegro feroce

51

W.W., Br., Ratchet

Strs., Tbns.

55

E Molto più mosso

59

Tpts.

Repeat only if necessary

Bs. Cl., Tbns.,
Vc., Cb.

63 Tutti (Tpts. continue)

216

END OF ACT TWO

25. Bows
Instrumental

Applause Segue

26. Exit Music
Instrumental

Art.